CHRISTIAN
POETRY

WATER
OF
GRACE

JEANNE DE CHANTAL TONDJE

Acknowledgments

I'm thankful to the LORD Jesus Christ, who gave me the grace to write this book. He gives the will and the doing.

I thank the servants of GOD who encouraged me to do this work.

I am deeply indebted to my husband and children, who have supported me throughout this journey. Their understanding, patience, and love have made this work possible.

TABLE OF CONTENTS

WATER OF GRACE

O rain, abundant rain,
You bring blessing to the earth.
Waters of grace, blessed waters,
On which GOD spoke through His Servants,
You have been a blessing for many.
Red Sea, you parted to make a way
For the people of Israel
While escaping to the promised land.
Bethesda Pool, you saw many sick people healed
When the angels troubled your waters.
Pool of Siloam, you witnessed the recovery
Of the sight of one born blind.
Jordan River, you saw a commander purified
From leprosy.
Wells of the ancient world,
You held the secrets of shepherds,
You held the secrets of travelers,
Who always found a resting place alongside you.
There was a particular well,
The well where JESUS sat after a journey,
Jacob's well.
Then came a Samaritan woman to draw water
For her usual domestic usage,
Without being aware of Who the Man was.
JESUS started a conversation about the physical water

that the woman placed her trust in;

His discussion then flowed to that of spiritual water

That only JESUS can give.

JESUS revealed to her who she was,

And then revealed to her Who HE IS

The fortunate woman understood

That she met the MESSIAH.

Convinced and believing,

She ran to town

To spread the great news.

She brought back with her a crowd,

The multitude that came

To see the MESSIAH,

Listening to HIM with their ears.

And believing in HIM,

received the living water

That quenches thirst forever,

The Words of Everlasting Life

Coming forth from the mouth

Of THE SAVIOR.

THE WATER OF GRACE

The grace of salvation

Fell upon the people of Sychar;

It was a great moment to be in that place.

Today, His GRACE is still available!

You do not even need to go to Jacob's well;
You need to turn your heart to JESUS
And believe in HIM.
For the water that HE gives will become
a fountain of living water within the believer,
Springing up into everlasting Life.
J. C. T.

THERE IS A MOUNTAIN!

Various mountains fill this world,
But there is a mountain
All people must explore.

Mount Sinai, the mount of the vision of fire:
You are significant; you bore the counsel
Of Israel, deliverance from bondage in Egypt.
You witnessed the handing over
Of the Decalogue
From GOD to Moses.
But there is another mountain that
needs to be explored.

Mount of Olives, you are blessed,
For the savior of the world
JESUS CHRIST raised mighty prayers
On you for this world.

There's still another mountain.

Mounts Ararat, you are kind,
You hosted Noah's Ark
And all the species that GOD
appointed to be preserved in the ark.
Species that populated the earth
After the flood.

But there is yet another mountain.

Mount Everest, you are
The highest Mountain in the world
Millions of tourists come
for exploration
Because of your elevation.
May your visitors see beyond your altitude
The Greatness of Your Maker,
GOD ALMIGHTY.

But there is yet still another mountain.

Explorers, mountain climbers
You are blameless,
Since you climb mountains
for your fitness
for the beauty of your physique.
But there's still a mountain
You need to climb for the beauty of your soul.
The Mountain from where come forth
Springs of living water:
Mount Zion,
Holy Mountain, the Mountain of GOD.
Mount Zion,

Mountain of your salvation.

Mount Zion,

Spiritual Mountain

Mount Zion

FOR THE BEAUTY OF YOUR SOUL

Mount Zion,

that you need to keep climbing.

J. C. T.

SOMETHING PRECIOUS

Great treasure
All people should long for
You were at the very beginning;
You will last forever;
You are worth more than precious metals,
More than pearls,
More than gold and silver.
You shine forth our Way;
You enlighten our Spirit;
You bring things to existence;
You are the truth, precious Word of GOD.
You reveal to us the will of GOD;
You are an incorruptible seed planted in our hearts;
You sanctify and cleanse us;
You are the sword of the Spirit.
Sharper than any two-edged sword,
On all battlefields,
You make us victors.
You are living and powerful,
Precious Word of GOD!
Blessed are the prophets of GOD,
Receiving revelations from The Holy Spirit,
And imparting them among people.
The man after the very heart of GOD,
King David understood the importance of the Word

And wrote the longest Psalm

Of the Bible on it, Psalm 119.

The commandments, the statutes,

And the law of GOD were his delights.

Precious Word, you lead us to eternal life.

Let us not merely read the Bible

as the book at our bedside!

Let us read it as the book of our hearts, mind, and soul.

Keeping the precepts and ordinances of God,

For it is written,

"This book of the law shall not depart

From your mouth, but you shall

Meditate on it day and night

That you may observe to do

accordingly to all that is written in it,

For then, you will make your Way

Prosperous, and then you will have

Good success,"

Joshua 1:8

J. C. T.

ADORATION

GOD is worthy to be praised!
O people! Where were you
before the foundation of this world?
Where were your memories
before you came into existence?
You can't attest to it, absolutely not,
Because you are but creatures.
Yet, there is a CREATOR
GOD ALMIGHTY,
Who created Heaven and Earth.
As a tree relies on its roots,
So, a house relies on its foundation.
We all depend on GOD,
"Know that THE LORD, HE is GOD;
It is HE who has made us,
and not we ourselves.
We are HIS people and
The sheep of His pasture."
Let's be his worshipers;
Let's worship Him in spirit and truth;
Let us sing praises to our LORD;
Let us sing a new song to GOD;
Let us lift His Holy NAME;
Let us bow down before HIM;
Let us worship THE LORD;

Let us praise Him with dancing;

Let our lives be those of worship;

Let us be grateful to HIM;

Let us bless HIS HOLY NAME!

Let's give thanks to HIM,

For His goodness, for His mercies,

For His great love, for His Grace

Worthy is THE LAMB of GOD!

J. C. T.

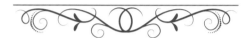

YOUR VOICE MATTERS

Romans 10:14,
"How then shall they call on Him
In Whom they have not believed?
And how shall they believe in Him
Of Whom they have not heard?
And how shall they hear without a preacher?"
The world needs more preachers!

Go into all the world,
And preach the Gospel.
It is a command from the LORD
The world is not far away;
The world is among us;
The world is people
who do not know THE LORD.
Without the knowledge of GOD
People are perishing.
Arise and preach the Gospel.
Apostle Paul said woe to him
If he is not preaching the Gospel!
Gospel preaching is your responsibility!
Let that be a priority
In your lifetime.
Your voice matters;
Your voice has an impact,

In the physical world

And in the spiritual.

The message of salvation that you carry

Will transform lives,

And people will be saved.

That message will cause repentance of the sinners,

And Heaven will rejoice!

Your voice matters.

Preaching the Gospel is a must.

Lazarus, being in the spiritual realm,

was begged to preach the Gospel

to the rich man's brothers.

But he could not come back after it was too late.

Bring GOD's message

During your earthly passage.

Your voice matters.

JESUS loves you;

JESUS died and rose again for you;

JESUS came to save you!

Let's hear these powerful utterances,

For none to be left behind

When the trumpet sounds.

Your voice matters.

As CHRIST's ambassador,

We appeal to your convictions,

That you put on boldness

And go into the world

To preach to the hopeless.

Your voice matters!

J. C. T.

FISHING

Mark 1:17,
"Then JESUS said to them,
'Follow ME, and I will make you
Become fishers of men.'"
JESUS CHRIST said fishers of men,
Not hunters of men!
Fishing is to win souls for CHRIST.
Fishing is to lead people to THE LORD.
And yet today, it appears there are
More hunters of men.
Crime is increasing;
Mass killings are happening;
Sicknesses and pandemics are arising;
Sin is increasing.
All these calamities are killing
And destroying people.
In their distress,
Don't let them be left hopeless:
Arise and preach the Gospel.
Without knowledge,
People are perishing.
Arise and cast your net!
Keep your shoes on,
For beautiful upon the mountains
Are the feet of those who bring good news!

Remember, you can fish for men with your faithful testimony.

Fish them with the Word of GOD.

Fish them up with prayers and fasting.

Fish them with good actions.

Fish them with a good reputation.

Within this generation,

We want to see the new "Apostle Peter" arising.

We want to see the new "Samaritan woman" rising.

We want to see the new "Rheinard Bonke" rising.

We want to see the new "Billy Graham." rising.

It's time to rise and diligently accomplish your mission.

Fulfill the Great Commission

For people to gain salvation.

J. C. T.

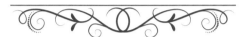

PRAYER, PRAYER, PRAYER

Momentous time of communication
With the Creator, GOD ALMIGHTY:
Our hearts long for this moment.
From THE LORD, we receive instruction.
That we should raise
Our voices and supplications
To make our requests known.
Let's seek the face of GOD.
Let's get onto our knees.
Let's climb the spiritual mountain.
Christians, stand your ground.
For the devil roars around,
Seeking whom to devour.
Let's declare and decree
to establish hedges of protection.
Let's knock for doors to be opened.
Let's seek to find good things.
Let's ask to receive.
Call on THE NAME OF THE LORD!
Address your first words of the day
to GOD, your maker.
recommend your morning.
recommend your day.
recommend your night
Into the Hands of THE LORD.

As Daniel, who prayed without ceasing,

Enter the upper room.

Everywhere, raise your pure hands.

Watch, pray, and call on THE LORD.

Be prayerful.

The KING OF KINGS set the example:

JESUS was always praying.

Even now, HE is interceding for us!

The ear of THE LORD is not deaf!

HE answers prayers.

GOD is looking for someone

To stand in the gap.

Intercede; intercede

For the land to be healed.

J. C. T.

NOBLE-MINDED PRINCESS

Coming from the land of your birth,
Going to a foreign land,

To an unknown place.

You did not go for exploration,

Nor to pursue happiness,

But to fill the gap of loneliness.

You went to accompany.

You did it for a just cause.

People knew your compassion.

People knew Your story.

You practiced what people were in desperate need of:

Love and true love.

You demonstrated true love

described In 1 Corinthians 13,

Not considering your youth,

Nor your interest,

You stood up to support

Ruth the Moabitess

Your mother-in-law.

You bore the seed of the fruit of the spirit,

And you displayed it to your surroundings.

The compassion and love

You demonstrated

Changed the bitter heart of

your Mother in law To a joyful one.

Women said you are more valuable

than sons numbering seven,

the number of perfection.

You perceived the meaning of true religion:

Taking care of widows and orphans.

You fulfilled the vows that you made.

In following your mother-in-law's destiny,

You made a declaration

That brought you to salvation.

Indeed, you came under

The wings of THE GOD of Israel,

Who is THE GOD of Naomi

THE CREATOR of the universe,

THE GOD who gives Eternal life.

You received blessings from above,

Entered the genealogy of King David,

The man after GOD's own heart.

Blessed are those who have true love,

For love is the fulfillment of the law.

Blessed are those who serve THE GOD of Israel.

J. C. T.

THE EGO

Ego, ego, you are a cunning deceiver!
As a bit of yeast works

through the whole batch of dough

 to make it rise,

You inflate the thoughts of man,

Making him proud.

You put him on a pedestal.

That was the way

you deceived all of Babel.

They conspired together.

they decided to construct a monument,

A tower that reaches to Heaven,

To make a name for themselves.

People of Babel, that was not the way:

GOD prepared the only Way through JESUS

for us to enter Heaven.

The people of Babel went astray

By seeking their way.

GOD said to go and multiply,

to cover the surface of the earth geographically.

But they wanted to redefine

their appointed mark on history,

To rebel against the plan of GOD,

To execute their project.

Did they not remember that GOD is Omniscient?

Did they not remember that GOD, the Almighty, is Omnipotent?

If THE LORD does not build the house,

Those who build are building in vain.

Ego, you caused the death of proud kings.

Ego, you turned a proud king into the mind of a beast.

The people of Babel did not realize

That seeking a reputation

would bring them confusion.

He who elevates himself will be brought low,

For GOD resists the proud.

The humble heart is a cherished virtue in the eyes of God.

J. C. T.

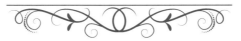

IT IS A JOURNEY!

O life, the existence of human beings.
Earthly life,

You are a journey:

You have your appointed time and then the end.

People have to depart

from this planet one day;

ancestors have gone;

They are no longer on Earth.

The bell tolls time-in for births

The bell tolls time-out for death

The knell rings from time to time

to announce departures from Earth.

Even those who lived

hundreds of years, nearly one thousand

like Methuselah,

had to depart from the Earth.

For there is a destination,

A final destination,

That GOD has prepared.

O man, where is your focus?

Your focal point should not be

On earthly things, they are temporal.

"The world is passing away,

and the lust of it, but he who

does the will of GOD abide forever."

That destination is spiritual.

No physical compass can lead you there.

No means of transportation

can lead you there.

There is a process

To reach that destination.

The secret is to walk with GOD,

Like Enoch and other saints did.

Today, you can walk with the HOLY SPIRIT,

Who leads in all truth

To come to believe in THE SON OF GOD, JESUS,

Walking according to the Bible,

According to the word of GOD.

Men of the Earth,

prepare to meet GOD,

By doing good,

By practicing justice,

By walking humbly before GOD.

Let your Spiritual eyes focus on Heaven.

J. C. T.

Made in United States
Troutdale, OR
08/08/2024